STREAMLINED

For Carrol Allen

This Is a Let's-Read-and-Find-Out Science Book

STREAMLINED

WRITTEN AND ILLUSTRATED BY JOHN KAUFMANN

THOMAS Y. CROWELL COMPANY   New York

LET'S-READ-AND-FIND-OUT SCIENCE BOOKS

Editors: **DR. ROMA GANS**, Professor Emeritus of Childhood Education, Teachers College, Columbia University
DR. FRANKLYN M. BRANLEY, Astronomer Emeritus and former Chairman of The American Museum-Hayden Planetarium

AIR, WATER, AND WEATHER
Air Is All Around You
The Clean Brook
Flash, Crash, Rumble, and Roll
Floating and Sinking
Icebergs
North, South, East, and West
Oxygen Keeps You Alive
Rain and Hail
Snow Is Falling
Sunshine Makes the Seasons
Water for Dinosaurs and You
Where the Brook Begins

THE EARTH AND ITS COMPOSITION
The Bottom of the Sea
Fossils Tell of Long Ago
Glaciers
A Map Is a Picture
Millions and Millions of Crystals
Salt
Where Does the Garbage Go?
The Wonder of Stones

ASTRONOMY AND SPACE
The Beginning of the Earth
The Big Dipper
Eclipse: Darkness in Daytime
The Moon Seems to Change
Rockets and Satellites
The Sun: Our Nearest Star
What Makes Day and Night
What the Moon Is Like*

MATTER AND ENERGY
Gravity Is a Mystery
High Sounds, Low Sounds
Hot as an Ice Cube
The Listening Walk
Streamlined
Upstairs and Downstairs
Weight and Weightlessness
What Makes a Shadow?

And other books on LIVING THINGS: PLANTS; LIVING THINGS: ANIMALS, BIRDS, FISH, INSECTS, etc.; and THE HUMAN BODY

*Available in Spanish

Copyright © 1974 by John Kaufmann.

All rights reserved. Except for use in a review, the reproduction or utilization of this work in any form or by any electronic, mechanical, or other means, now known or hereafter invented, including xerography, photocopying, and recording, and in any information storage and retrieval system is forbidden without the written permission of the publisher. Published simultaneously in Canada by Fitzhenry & Whiteside Limited, Toronto. Manufactured in the United States of America. ISBN 0-690-00273-4   0-690-00565-2 (LB)

Library of Congress Cataloging in Publication Data Kaufmann, John. Streamlined. (Let's-read-and-find-out science book) SUMMARY: Discusses in simple terms, with examples from nature and technology, the effects of shape on the speed and efficiency of movement through air and water. 1. Aerodynamics–Juv. lit. 2. Fluid dynamics–Juv. lit. [1. Aerodynamics. 2. Fluid dynamics. I. Title. QA930.K36   532'.05   74-2357   ISBN 0-690-00273-4   ISBN 0-690-00565-2(lib. bdg.)

1   2   3   4   5   6   7   8   9   10

STREAMLINED

Slim, sleek, stumpy, flat, round, pointy—animals come in different shapes. The shape of an animal tells something about how it moves.

A hippopotamus has a big, fat, lumpy body. It looks very slow—and it is.

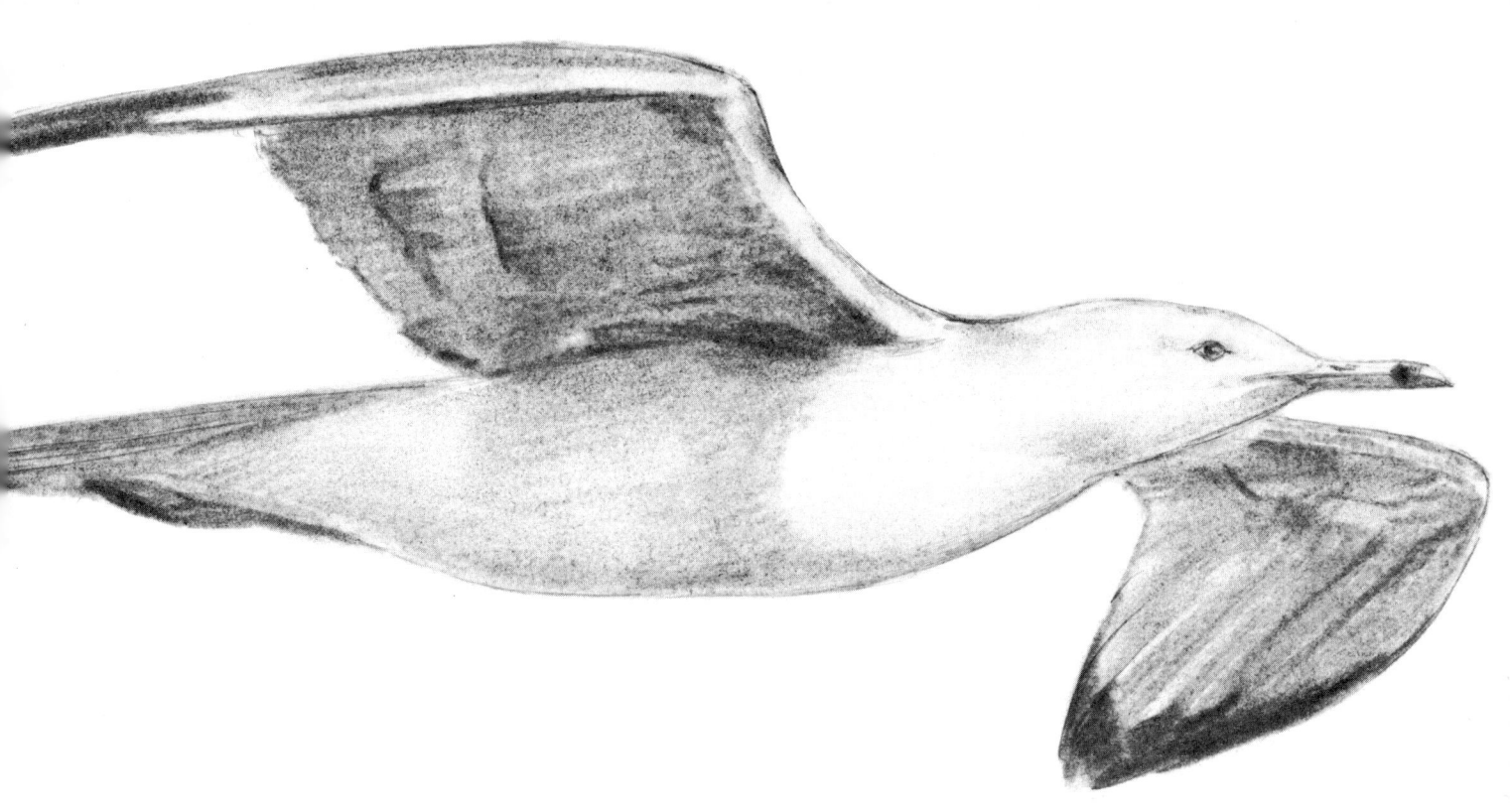

Other animals look fast. The bodies of birds are shaped for speed. A seagull's body is slender and curved to move easily through the air. A gull flies swiftly and hardly seems to work at all.

Seals are also shaped for speed. The body of a seal is curved to pass smoothly through the water. The seal streaks along with easy strokes of its flippers. It usually swims upside down and searches below for fish to eat.

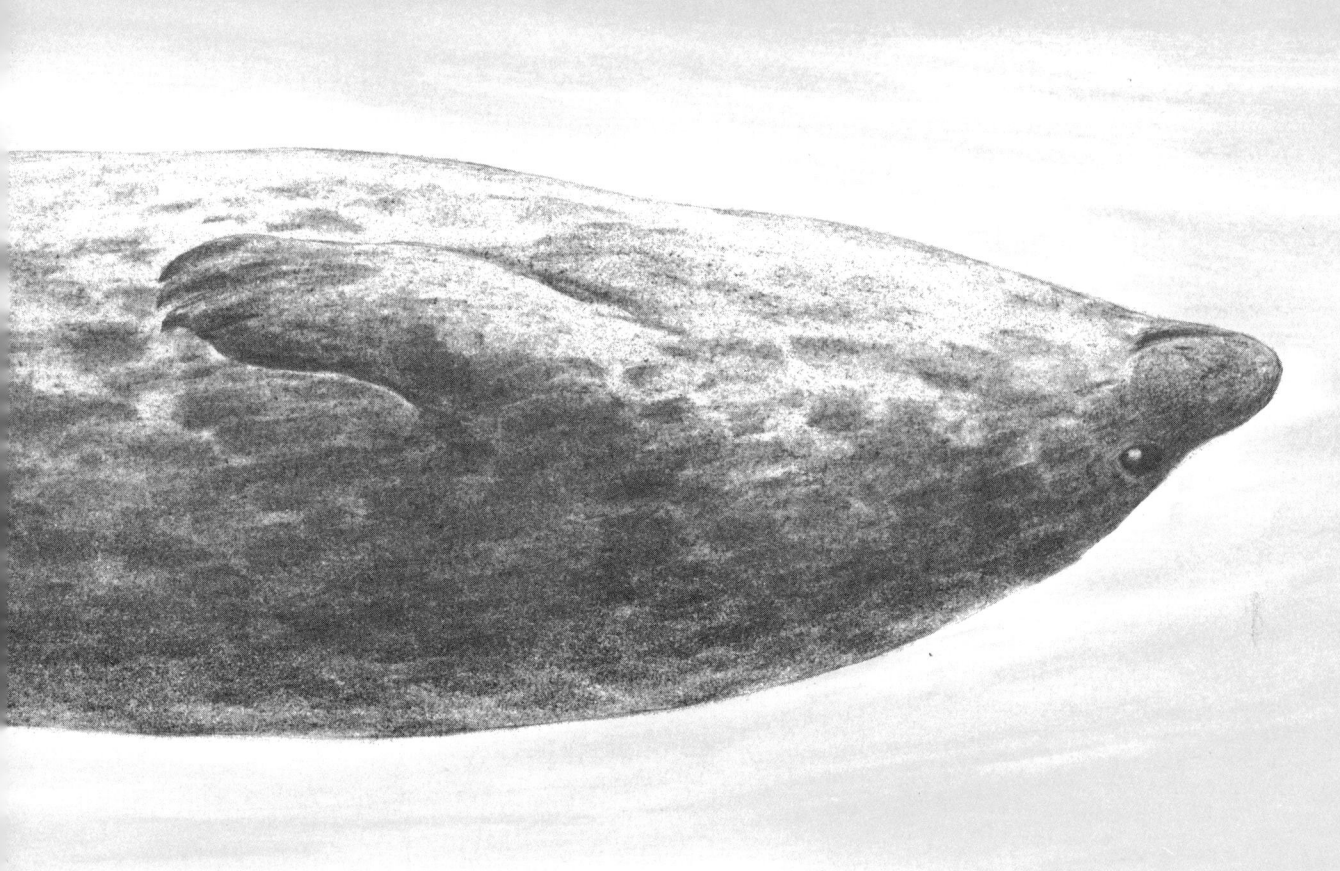

Flying gull and swimming seal—one moves through the air, and the other through the water.

When a bird moves through air, the air spreads apart, passes around it, then flows together again.

When a fish or a seal moves through water, the water also spreads apart, streams past, and flows together.

When the shape of something allows air or water to pass by smoothly, it is streamlined.

Many animals are streamlined. Their heads are curved or pointed. Their curving bodies slim down toward their tails. Birds, bats, fish, seals, otters, beavers, and many other creatures are shaped this way.

Many man-made things are also streamlined. Airplane bodies are smoothly curved to move quickly and easily through the air.

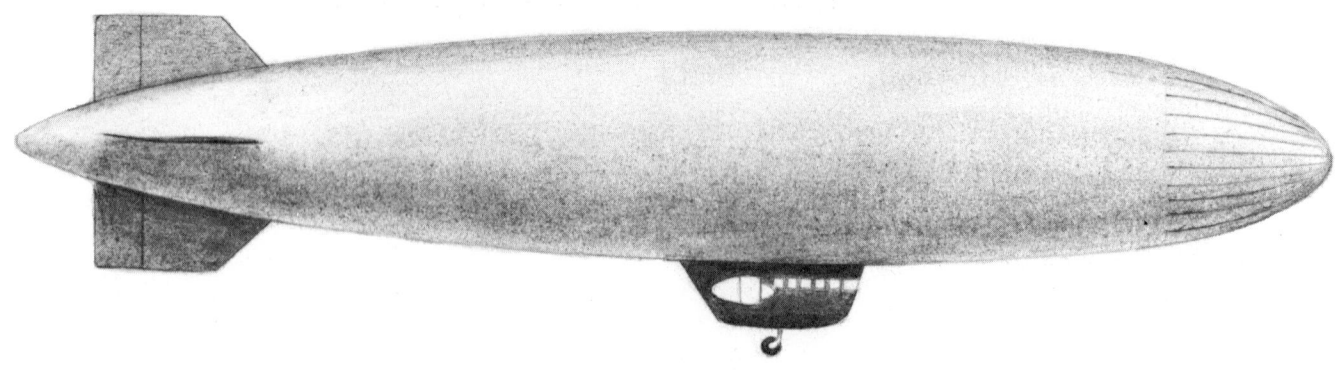

Blimps are streamlined.

So are racing cars and high-speed trains.

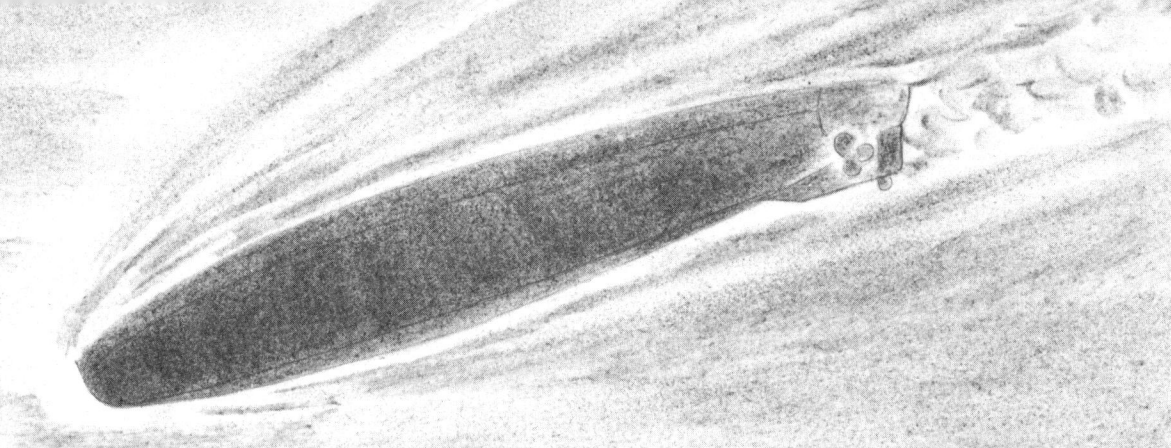

Boats are streamlined to pass easily through water. Submarines travel under water. Their hulls are long and curving like the bodies of seals and dolphins.

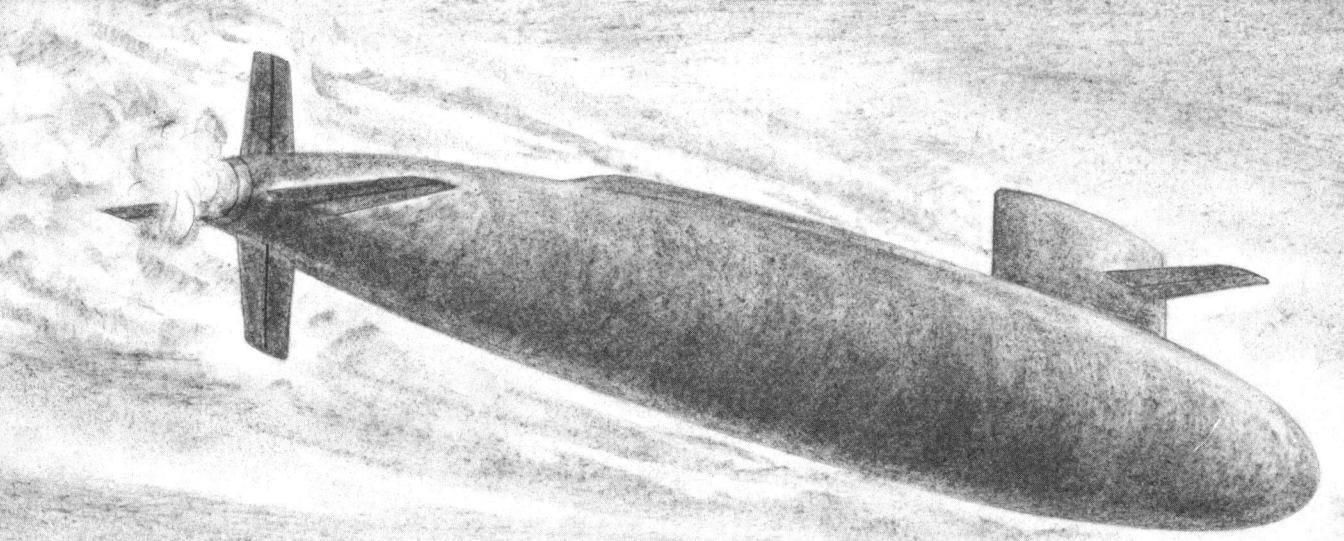

Birds, seals, planes, submarines are all streamlined. They all have the same special kind of shape. This shape is called a teardrop.

Let's do some experiments to see what happens when teardrops and other shapes move through water or air.

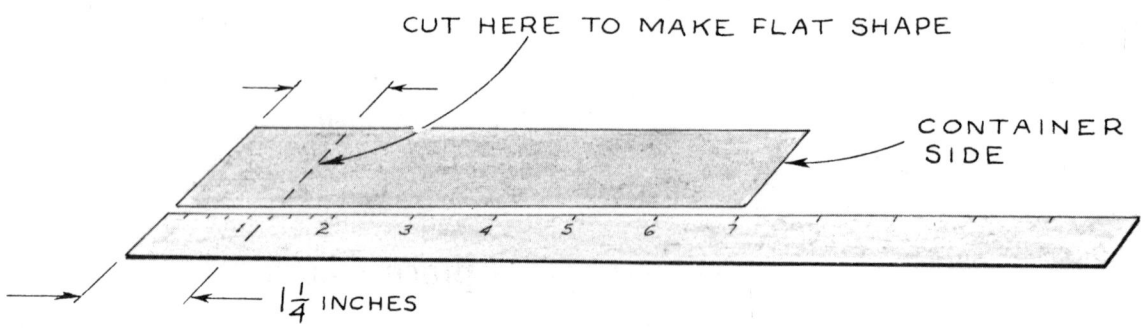

Start with an empty milk container. Cut out three sides. Make the three shapes as the pictures show.

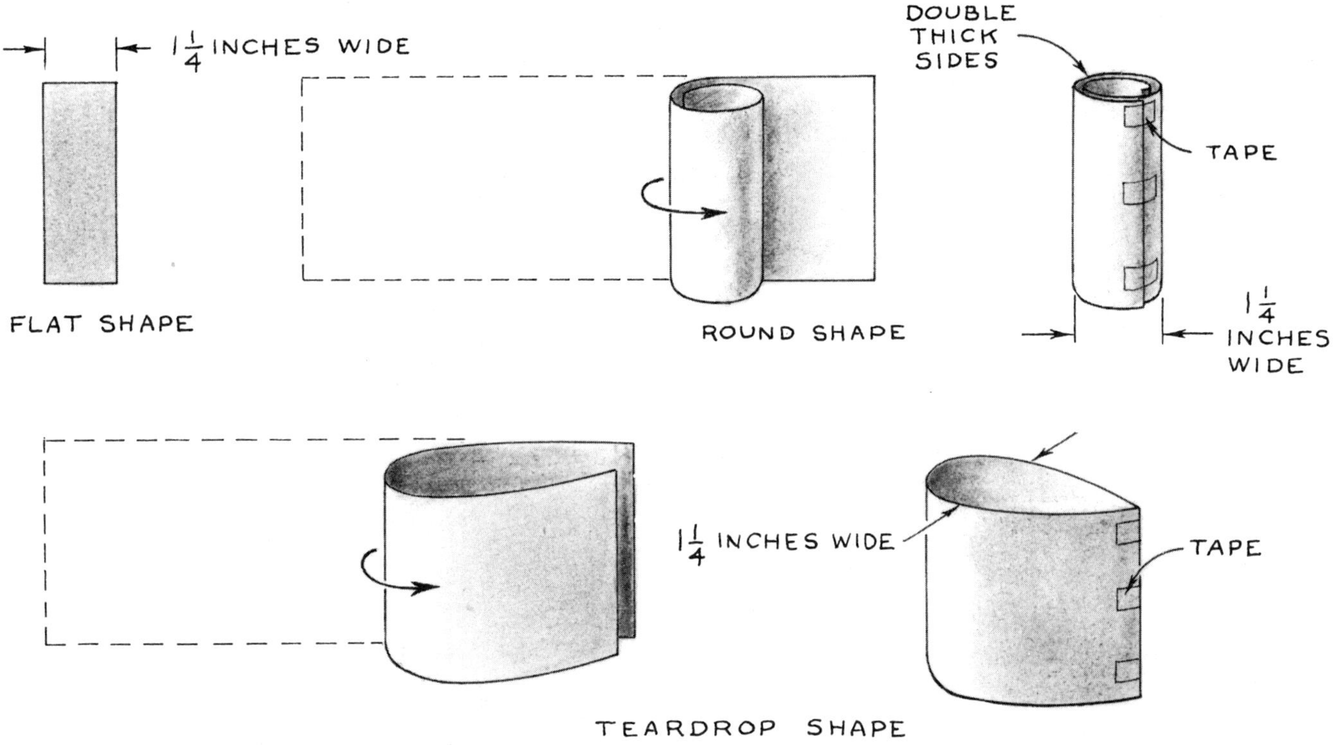

Leave the first piece flat. Form the second piece into a round shape. Bend the third piece into a teardrop shape. With thumbtacks fasten each shape to a stick or a pencil.

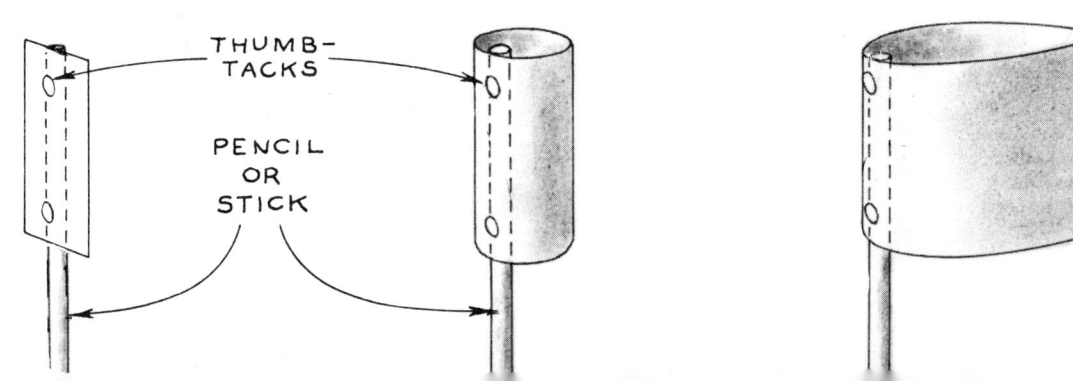

Next, put a few inches of water into your bathtub. Move the teardrop shape through the water. Try it with the pointed end in front and then with the curved end in front. Which way does it move more easily? Think of the way seals and submarines move.

Watch how the water flows around the flat shape, the round shape, and the teardrop shape. Which one causes just a few small ripples? Which causes a lot of ripples?

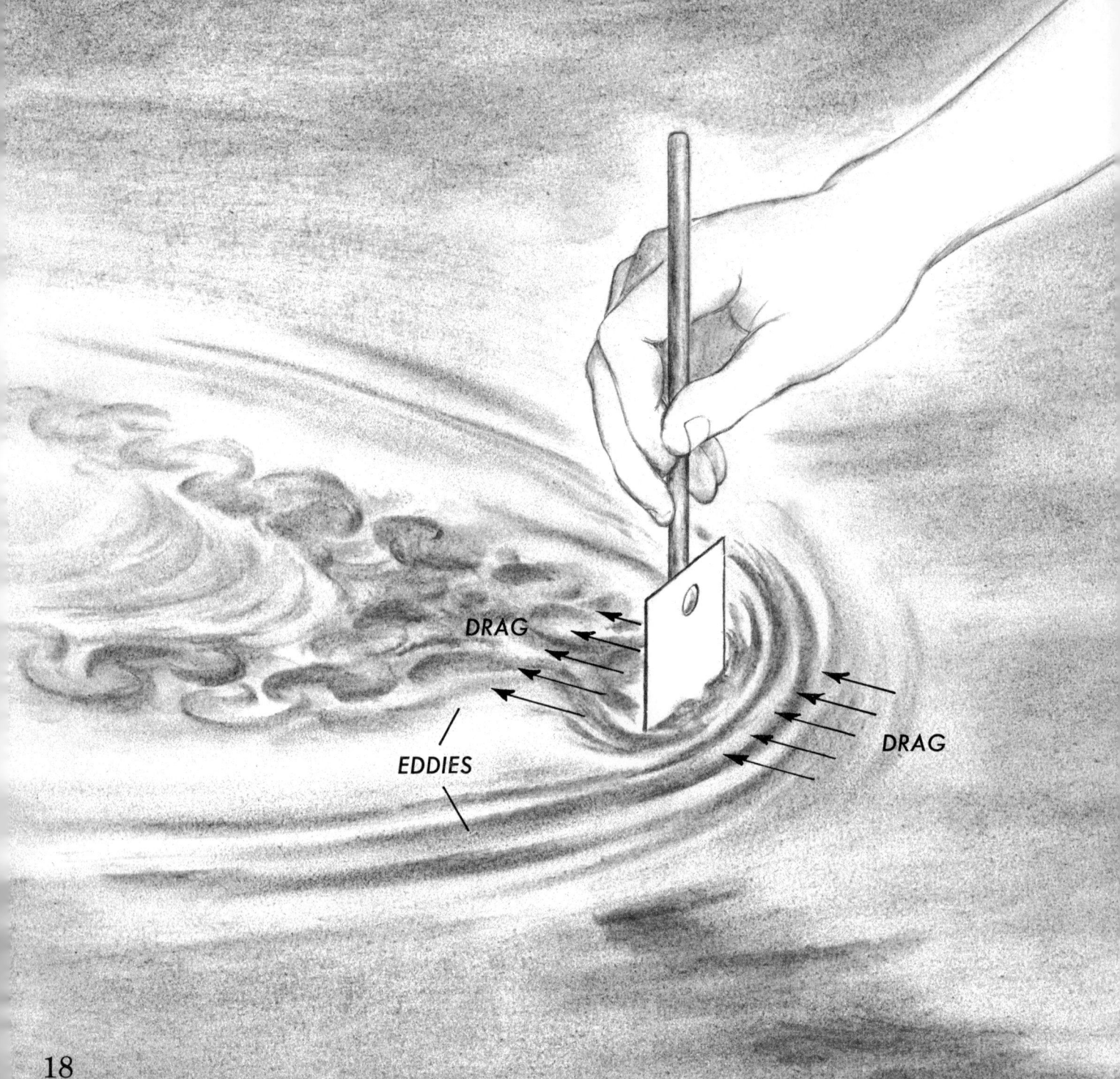

Here is what happens. When you put the flat cardboard in water, the push on the front of it is the same as the push on the back of it. When you move the cardboard through water, it makes a lot of ripples called eddies. The push on the front of the cardboard is now more than the push on the back. The push toward the back of the cardboard is called drag. A flat shape causes a lot of drag.

At higher speeds the drag becomes very strong. Pull the flat shape through the water fast. You can feel how hard it is to move it. The water in front of it is pushed way out to the sides, making big, rough eddies. Because it causes so much drag, a flat shape is no good for anything that must move fast through water or air.

The front of the round shape spreads the water apart more smoothly. The side eddies are much smaller than those of the flat shape.

The round shape has less drag. The push in front is more nearly the same as the push in back, so it is easier to move it through the water. But strong eddies curl in behind the round shape, too. It is not the best shape for anything moving fast in the water or the air.

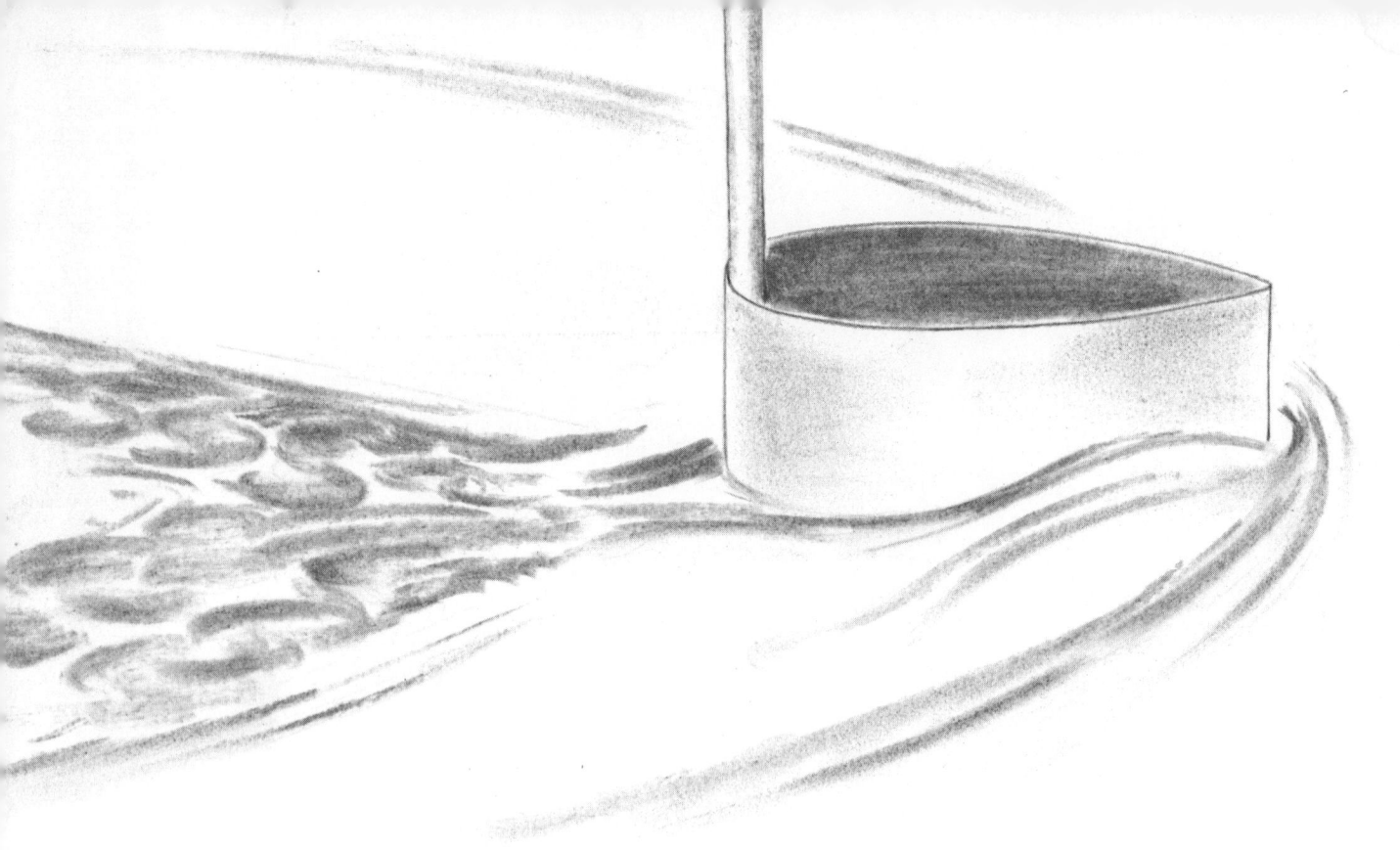

When you move the teardrop shape the wrong way, with its point in front, it is not much better than the round shape. Although its sharp point cuts a path through the water, its rounded back forms large eddies. They cause a lot of drag.

When you move it the right way, with its curved end in front, the teardrop shape makes a smooth path. Its curved and pointed body keeps the eddies small. There is very little drag. The push in front and back is just about the same.

At high speed a teardrop shape still causes very little drag. Hold the teardrop shape under a faucet, rounded end up. Turn the water on. Even when you run it very fast, the water streams smoothly over the teardrop shape. This shape is more perfectly streamlined than any other.

Fast-moving animals, birds, and fish have bodies that look like teardrop shapes. People who design racing cars, rockets, submarines, and other things that must move quickly and easily through air or water also use the teardrop shape. It is the best possible kind of shape for anything moving fast through water or air.

Now try the three shapes in air. Hold them outdoors against the wind or indoors in front of a fan.

Air is invisible. We cannot see it. You cannot watch it flow the way you can watch water. But you can feel how hard the air pushes back on the flat, the round, and the teardrop shapes. As it does in water, the teardrop gives the least drag.

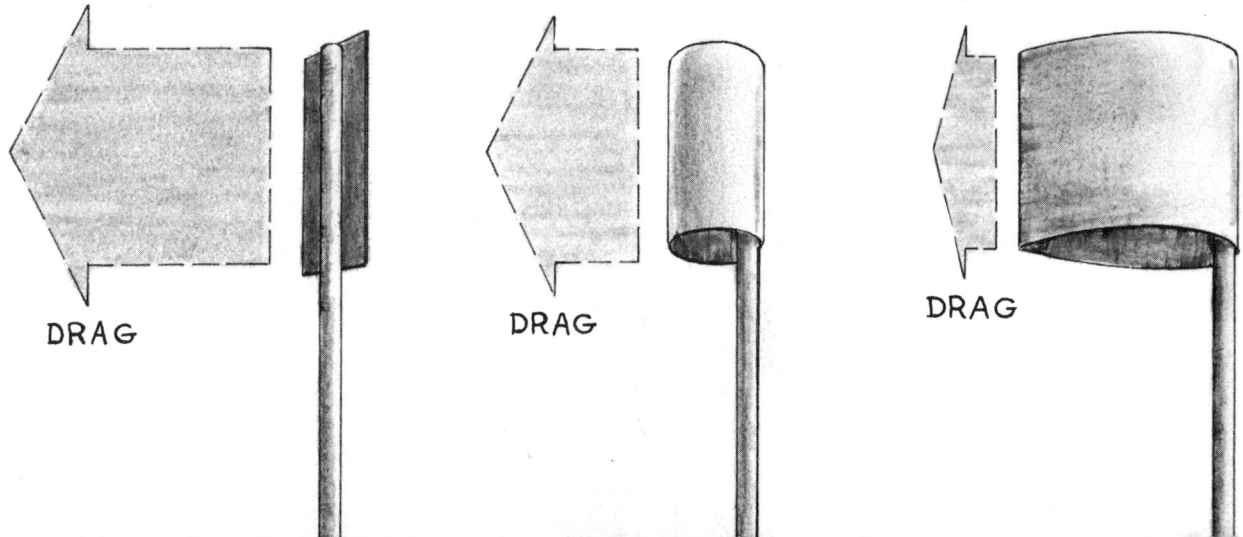

Streamlined things are usually smooth, too. Smoothness causes less drag. The feathers of birds, the scales of fish, the skin of dolphins, and the hair of seals are smooth coverings for their streamlined bodies. Airplanes, boats, cars, and trains also have smooth outer skins.

SIDE VIEW

TOP VIEW

Some streamlined things are not rounded teardrop shapes like the body of a bird or an airplane. Racing cars are streamlined only one way. So are many fish. If you look at those fish from the side, or at those racing cars from above, they don't look streamlined.

TOP VIEW

SIDE VIEW

Some things that move extremely fast are not streamlined at all. Spacecraft have parts that stick out all over. There is no air in outer space to cause drag and slow the spacecraft down, so their shape does not matter.

But the rockets that blast spacecraft from the earth are streamlined. They have to travel very fast through the air.

Streamlining makes it easier for animals and machines to move fast and far. Streamlined animals use less muscle power and less body fuel. They can travel farther on the fuel they have. Some birds can fly day and night more than two thousand miles without stopping.

Streamlining also makes planes, cars, boats, trains, and rockets use less engine power and less fuel. They too can travel farther. Some jet airliners can fly several thousand miles nonstop in half a day.

Look at fish, cars, birds, airplanes, all kinds of animals. Some of them move very quickly and easily, using as little power and fuel as possible. You can tell which ones they are by their shape. They are shaped for speed. They are streamlined.

ABOUT THE AUTHOR / ILLUSTRATOR

John Kaufmann has written and illustrated many books for children, several of which have dealt with different aspects of the principles of flight. His previous title in the Let's-Read-and-Find-Out series was *Bats in the Dark*, and for older readers he has written *Robins Fly North, Robins Fly South*.

Mr. Kaufmann lives in Fresh Meadows, New York, with his wife, Alicia, who is also a writer, and their two sons, Darius and Noel.